Noël Greig

Noël has worked in theatre since 1966 as an actor, director, playwright and dramaturge. Companies with whom he has had a major involvement include: The Brighton Combination, Inter Action, The General Will, Gay Sweatshop, The Oval House, Red Ladder, Nottingham Roundabout Theatre, The Crucible Theatre Sheffield, Deal Theatre Project, Birmingham Rep, Leicester Haymarket Theatre, The Royal Court, Contact Theatre Manchester, Pursued by a Bear and Theatre Centre. *Trashed* is his eighth play for Theatre Centre. He also works regularly overseas. Routledge have recently published a book containing all the work he does with writers and writers' workshops: *Playwriting. A Practical Guide*.

For Rosamunde Hutt

THEATRE CENTRE

presents

Trashed

by

Noël Greig

AURORA METRO PRESS

First printed in 2004 by Aurora Metro Publications Ltd.
www.aurorametro.com Tel: 020 8747 1953

With thanks to the staff at Theatre Centre, Thomas Kell, Rhona Foulis.

Trade distribution:
UK - Central Books Tel: 020 8986 4854 Fax: 020 8533 5821
USA - Theatre Communications Group, N.Y. Tel: 212 609 5900
Canada - Playwrights Union of Canada Tel: 416 703 0013
Printed by IntypeLibra, Wimbledon, UK
ISBN 978-09546912-2-9

THEATRE CENTRE

Trashed is Theatre Centre's first play in its second half century! In 2003, the company celebrated 50 years of commissioning, producing and touring new drama for young people. The work offered during the year reflected the breadth of the company's mission and reach: hard-edged contemporary writing for teenagers by Angela Turvey (*Precious*) and Manjinder Virk (*Glow*) sat alongside a new production, created with Manchester's Royal Exchange Theatre, of Charles Way's classic and enchanting *A Spell of Cold Weather* for our youngest audiences and their families; Rosy Fordham's unsettling *Missing* brought a sophisticated theatrical sensibility into junior school halls whilst *Reality Check*, written by the company's teenage Young Apprentice writers from Tower Hamlets in London, saw the newest voices in British Theatre professionally produced and warmly received.

Together with Aurora Metro, the company published a significant Anthology of recent plays for teenagers (including *Glow* and *Precious* as well as writing by Roy Williams, Anna Reynolds, Benjamin Zephaniah and Anna Furse) titled *Theatre Centre: plays for young people*.

In the Autumn of 2004, Theatre Centre renews its relationship with the Sherman Theatre, Cardiff, as a co-producer on Mike Kenny's *One Dark Night*. Playwright Sarah Woods has been commissioned to create *Walking on Water* for learning disabled audiences, the fruit of the company's collaboration with Full Body and the Voice.

In 2006, the company will join Unicorn Theatre to present an adaptation by Carl Miller of Eva Ibbotson's acclaimed novel *Journey to the River Sea* in the new Unicorn Theatre on London's South Bank and subsequently on national tour.

THEATRE CENTRE

Founder Patron
Brian Way

Patrons for the 50th Birthday Year
Bonnie Greer G. Laurence Harbottle
Diane Louise Jordan Benjamin Zephaniah

Honorary Advisors
Stuart Bennett Geoff Bullen Patrick Boyd Maunsell

Members of the Board of Directors
Hazel Durrant Irene Macdonald *(Chair)*
Saifur Rahman Pat Trueman Roy Williams

Members of Staff
Rosamunde Hutt *(Director)*

Charles Bishop *(General Manager/Deputy Director)*
Louisa Charles *(Finance Manager (Freelance))*
Lesley Jones *(Domestic)*
Michael Judge *(Associate Artist (Education))*
Thomas Kell *(Administrator/Deputy General Manager)*
Marijke Zwart *(Production Manager/Company Stage Manager)*

Associate Artists
William Elliott Lawrence Evans Jane Mackintosh
Paul J. Medford Bernadette O'Brien

Units 7 & 8, Toynbee Workshops,
3 Gunthorpe Street,
London E1 7RQ
Tel.: 020 7377 0379
Fax.: 020 7377 1376
admin@theatre-centre.co.uk
www.theatre-centre.co.uk

Trashed

by Noël Greig

Rupi Lal – Abs
Louise Mohammed – Ruhela
Andrew Sykes – Mel
Anstey Thomas – Louisa

Co-Director: Noël Greig
Co-Director/Dramaturge: Michael Judge
Designer: Rachana Jadhav
Composer: Hettie Malcomson, in collaboration with Catherine Shrubshall
Lighting Designer: Ceri James
Accent Advice: Jan Haydn Rowles
Casting and Voice Advice: Bernadette O'Brien
Production Manager and Company Stage Manager: Marijke Zwart
Production Assistant: Marina Hadjipanayi
Set Builder: Mark Wilson at Set-Up (Scenery) Ltd
Education Resources: Michael Judge
Graphic Design: David Bradshaw
Production Photography: Hugo Glendinning

Writer's Note:
The genesis of *Trashed* goes back to 1997 when Rosamunde Hutt directed my play *Common Heaven* for the company. The collaboration with Ros was so rich and rewarding that, when I was asked to write for Theatre Centre again, my one condition was that this collaboration should be continued. For the past 18 months, Ros has encouraged and supported the development of the play and, in a try-out week in June, she began to uncover the manner in which it should take final shape on stage. Although Ros had to withdraw from directing the production of *Trashed*, her guiding intellect and spirit has been at the heart of the process throughout, as a full part of the team.

Noël Greig

Biographies

Rupi Lal – Abs

Photo: Claire Grogan

Rupi began his acting career in youth productions at the Old Rep Theatre with the Birmingham Theatre School, most notably playing the role of the Creature in Mary Shelley's *Frankenstein*. At eighteen, he made his television début in the BBC children's programme, *Brum*. His most recent television work was a commercial for Computeach. Rupi has just completed a BA Honours degree in Acting from Rose Bruford College of Speech and Drama, achieving a distinction in stage combat. *Trashed* marks Rupi's début with Theatre Centre.

Louise Mohammed – Ruhela

Photo: Richard Blower

Born in London, Louise is of mixed race parents. At an early age, she felt a love for the theatre and after leaving school studied at the Guildford School of Acting. In her three years there, she played such diverse roles as Julie in *Ripen Our Darkness* and an Old Lady in *The Dining Room*. Since leaving college, she has worked extensively in Theatre in Education with companies such as Caught in the Act, Crag Rats and Raised Eyebrow. In her spare time, Louise enjoys Tae Kwondo, driving and pulling pints at her local pub.

Andrew Sykes – Mel

Photo: Matt Stoney

Andrew graduated from Rose Bruford College in 2002. His professional theatre credits include: *The Bright and Bold Design*, *The Marlboro Man* and *Someone is going to come*. Theatre in training includes: *The Seagull*, *Othello*, *Dogs Barking*, *Princess Ivona* and *Much Ado About Nothing*. Andy has also set up his own theatre company, Theatre Test Tube, who most recently performed at Hull Truck Theatre. Television credits include: *The Impressionable John Culshaw* (ITV) and *The Dambusters* (Channel Four).

Anstey Thomas – Louisa

Photo: Chris Baker

Anstey studied English/Drama at London University and then trained at The Poor School. Theatre includes: *A Doll's House* (Wild Iris) Oslo Ibsen Festival; Yelena in *The Red Princess* (Red Shift); *Dr Faustus* (Kaos Theatre); Gillian in *Big Burger Chronicles* (Theatre Absolute/ Belgrade Coventry); Aphrodite in *Hippolytos* (Theatre Melange); the witch in *Hansel and Gretel* (Forest Forge); *Sell Out* (Frantic Assembly); the Artful Dodger in *Oliver Twist* (TNT/ American Drama Group of Europe) national tour; Doreen Rash in *Tithe War* and Old Miriam in *The Edge of the Land* (both Eastern Angles); George in *You've fingered it and now you've got to eat it...* (Jammy Tarts) at the Pleasance, Edinburgh.

Noël Greig – Writer and Co-Director

(see biography on page one)

Michael Judge – Co-Director/Dramaturge

Michael studied with Philippe Gaulier and Monica Pagneux and at the Central School of Speech and Drama. He began professional life directing at the Minerva Studio Theatre. He has been Assistant Director to Sam Mendes and Michael Bogdanov on various plays, including *Love's Labours Lost* and *The Cherry Orchard*. As a drama teacher in the East End of London, Michael directed touring productions of *Oroonoko*, *Brick Lane Balti* and *Kane and the Sea of Stories*. He is the Associate Artist for Education at Theatre Centre, with whom he initiated the *Authentic Voices* programme and co-directed *Reality Check*, with Noël Greig, in 2003.

Rachana Jadhav – Designer

After graduating as an Architect from Edinburgh College of Art, Rachana completed an MA in Scenography at Central Saint Martin's in 2002. Since then she has been involved in theatre, designing set and costume for: *Miss Julie* (Naach Theatre Company, 2003); *Dancing within Walls* and *Curry Tales* (RASA Productions, 2003/2004); *Slam Dunk* (Nitro Theatre Co., 2004); and *The Greatest Drummer in the World* (Ensemble, 2004). Rachana exhibits as an installation artist, and after co-founding Naach in 2003 with director Nadia Fall, is currently preparing new devised work for 2005.

Hettie Malcomson – Composer

As a music composer, Hettie's work for theatre includes: *Jumping on my Shadow* (Theatre Centre); *As You Like It* (Sphinx); *Cinderella* (London Bubble); and *Mushroom Man* (Hungry Grass). Film and television work includes: *Ice Girls* (BBC, CTV); *Roy* (CBC); *One More Push* (Channel 4); *The Second Bakery Attack* (Sundance & London Film Festivals); and *From the Ashes* (Channel 4). Hettie's concert performances include the Spitalfields and Bath Festivals, and broadcasts on Radio 3.

Ceri James – Lighting Designer
Ceri trained at the Welsh College of Music and Drama and the University of Southern California. He has worked as a Lighting Designer for the past 12 years. Recent credits include: *As You Like It* and *Twelfth Night* (both Mappa Mundi Theatre); *Dreaming Amelia* and *Angels Don't Need Wings* (Hijinx Theatre); *The Little Prince* and *Bowled a Googly* (Oxfordshire Touring Theatre Company); *Babe* (Sherman Theatre Company); *Music Makers* & *Movie Awards* (BBC and the National Orchestra of Wales); *Echoes in the Stones*, for Tintern Abbey Son-et-Lumière Festival; and *Much Ado About Nothing*, for Caerphilly Festival. Ceri has worked for Theatre Centre as Lighting Designer for *Under the Bed*, *Pork Bellies*, *Precious* and *Glow*.

Marijke Zwart – Production Manager / Company Stage Manager
Marijke was born in the Netherlands, where she worked with Natasha Emanuëls and Panther Theatre Company. In England, she has worked for: Dorothy Talk Theatre Company, Gay Sweatshop, Ruby Tuesday Productions, Pilot Theatre Company, the Hungry Grass Theatre Company and on various productions at the Drill Hall in London. She designed lighting for the Isadora Duncan Dance Group and for the Gay Sweatshop productions *Club Bent* and *Club Deviance*. In 2000, Marijke won the Stage Management Association Stage Manager of the Year Award for her contribution to *Gorgeous* by Anna Furse (Theatre Centre).

Rosamunde Hutt – Theatre Centre Director
Rosamunde has worked extensively in theatre since 1978. As resident Director of Theatre Centre since 1993, she has commissioned over 30 new plays, directing most recently, *Precious* by Angela Turvey and *A Spell of Cold Weather* by Charles Way. Her production of *Gorgeous* by Anna Furse toured to the Philippines and Kuala Lumpur and she re-directed Theatre Centre's production of *Breaking China* by Fiona Graham for the Act 3 Children's

First Festival in 2003, with a Singaporean cast. Rosamunde has also worked for Spectacle Theatre, the Sherman Theatre Company, Belgrade TIE Coventry, Hijinx Theatre (with whom she was associated for 8 years) and Polka Theatre for Children, directing *The Secret Garden* (adapted by Neil Duffield). Other directing credits include: *Mushroom Man* by Hannah Beecham for adult audiences (Hungry Grass Theatre Company) and, in 2004, *Dragon Breath* by Peter Rumney (whose Theatre Centre commission *Jumping on My Shadow* won the 2002 John Whiting Award) for Made to Measure / Creative Partnerships, Nottingham.

We would like to thank all the following people who helped us develop *Trashed*:
Tanya Franks, Colin Kilbride, Hema Mangoo and Keith Saha; Towhida Afsar (and her mother Hena and brother Ivan) and all the other Young Apprentice Writers: Nasmia Begum, Dilruba Begum, Rahima Begum, Sophie Bowman, Shirin Hirsch, Fahima Nessa, Holly Samson, Tunde Sanusi; the cast (Kiran Dadlani, Hema Mangoo, Keith Saha, Amit Sharma, Karen Spicer) and creators of *Reality Check*; teachers and students at Hainault Forest and St Paul's Way Schools in London and Baylis Court School in Slough; Slough Creative Partnerships; Connect 5 (Excellence in Cities); Meredith Fruchtman; Cathy Ryan.

Introduction

In the months after 9/11, I was working on the *Authentic Voices* new writing project at Theatre Centre. It was an opportunity for young writers in the East End to write their own stories in response to two Theatre Centre plays, *Jumping On My Shadow* by Peter Rumney and *Souls* by Roy Williams. One story was particularly resonant: a young Bangladeshi girl wrote about her uncle, who she visited in New York. The family had made a trip to Coney Island beach on a day with clear blue skies. Her uncle worked in IT on the 300th floor of the World Trade Centre; he died when the second tower collapsed. The girl's writing articulated her loss. In this post–9/11 era, as the media is full of Islamophobia and talk of irreconcilable differences of culture, it is in our losses that we share the most.

The work of the *Authentic Voices* writers was toured back to their schools in a professional production, *Reality Check*. Noël Greig worked closely with me on the project, his imagination watered by the young writers. The footprints and the ghosts of their stories are in *Trashed*: the losses of 9/11, a fifteen year old Bengali Bride, a jogger in an East End Park, a young Muslim called Abs, a jellyfish on Coney Island Beach, a young Muslim girl imagining the multitude of parallel lives that could exist in the universe, an East End couple facing the reality of death, a young girl who wants to develop her musical talents against her parents' wishes. When *Trashed* tours, the young writers will pen their responses, opening up the dialectical nature of theatre: for every thesis, an antithesis. In Rustom Bharucha's words, "when the play ends what begins?"

Michael Judge
Associate Artist (Education) at Theatre Centre
Co-Director and Dramaturge, *Trashed*

Trashed

There were a number of inspirations that led to the story of *Trashed*. A major one was the woman in the USA who, interviewed on TV immediately after the 9/11 attacks (in which she had lost a loved one), said that she did not want the government to take any revenge on her behalf. Not surprisingly, that interview was swiftly buried and never shown again. There were also the conversations I have had with young Muslim women in London, Syria and Jordan concerning the hijab and what it represents to them. I was also interested to see what would happen if two women from extremely different (and seemingly opposing) cultures were thrown together in a moment of crisis. In this 'globalised' world, can we (and how do we) accommodate the 'other' and still retain our own sense of identity?

Noël Greig

Trashed

Noël Greig

First performed at Redbridge Drama Centre, London E18 on 23rd September, 2004.

Characters

RUHELA British Asian (Bengali). In the London scenes she is sixteen. In the New York scenes she is thirteen.

LOUISA White American, in her forties. She retains the accent of her Mississippi upbringing.

ABS Ruhela's brother. In his early-to-mid twenties.

MEL Louisa's son. In his early-to-mid twenties. He speaks with a New York accent.

Writer's Notes:

A thought unfinished is indicated by...

A thought interrupted by another speaker is indicated by/

When / appears between CHARACTER NAMES it indicates that the following line or lines are spoken by all characters. For example:

LOUISA/ABS It won't, it won't come here.

[In translation: indicates that the following passage is spoken in the Bangladeshi dialect of Sylheti.]

At points during the action, RUHELA will loosen her hijab, so that it is resting on her shoulders. At other points she will adjust it to cover her head. She never takes it off completely. The major moments of use – to disclose or cover up – are indicated in the text, but the rehearsal process will discover other significant moments.

The play takes place in London, September 2004, and New York, September 2001.

London. 2004.
The faint sound of thunder in the distance.
The sound of police sirens in the middle-distance.

RUHELA enters. She wears a hijab, with a long skirt and trainers. She has a bag, in which is a portable CD player. She is eating from a carton of McDonald's fries.

The faint sound of thunder again, in the distance. The sound of leaves rustling in the breeze. RUHELA looks up. She puts in her earphones and presses 'play' on the CD. Music: the opening of Dvořák's 'New World' Symphony. A phone rings. The music and the breeze and the wind fade. RUHELA listens to the conversation (it is in her memory).

FEMALE VOICE 1 Salem alekum.
FEMALE VOICE 2 Is Ruhela there? Is this the number for Ruhela? [Pronounced as Roo-hay-la]
FEMALE VOICE 1 [In translation, off phone: Eh Ruhela, [Pronounced as Roo-hell-a] Son of Miah, eh. Son of Miah. Come here, come here.]
MALE VOICE [In translation, off phone: Who is it?]
FEMALE VOICE 1 [In translation: What has my daughter been doing? Is she in trouble?]
FEMALE VOICE 2 I'm sorry, but I don't under/

FEMALE VOICE 1 [In translation, off phone: Come here, come here, hurry up.]

MALE VOICE Salem alekum. How may I help? *(Pause)* You wish to speak to my daughter? [In translation, off phone: Ruhela! Ruhela... you are wanted on the phone.] Who shall I say is calling?

FEMALE VOICE 2 Louisa. Tell her it is Louisa Mydell, and I would like to...

The voice fades out as the sound of sirens and traffic fades in.

London, one week after the phone call.
The sound of police sirens and traffic in the distance.
It is early autumn. We are in a small run-down park. There is a mesh fence surrounding it. Caught in the mesh are leaves and rubbish: plastic bags, a Cross of St George flag, newsprint etc. The ground is strewn with litter. The leaves rustle in the light breeze.

RUHELA is still listening to her CD (we do not hear it), and eating from her McDonald's carton. A jogger (it is RUHELA'S memory of ABS) enters. He stops near to RUHELA and does some exercises. Having completed his exercises, he exits, running.

RUHELA looks around her again, then looks at her watch. She waves her finger in time to the music she is listening to. She looks at her watch again, then takes out her mobile phone. She looks at her messages. There are none. She puts the phone away and continues listening to the music.
LOUISA enters. She has blonde hair (assisted, these days). Her style of dress is on the 'flashy' side and she is wearing high heels. She has a shoulder bag and a heavy travelling case. One of its wheels has dropped off, so she has to carry it. She stops, puts the case down and draws breath a few times. She coughs from her chest for a moment. She sees RUHELA, picks up her case, with some effort, and crosses towards her.

LOUISA Ruhela? [Pronounced as Roo-hay-lah] *(RUHELA is listening to her music and does not hear or see her.)* Ruhela!
(RUHELA sees LOUISA. She turns off her CD player and takes off her earphones.)
Hi. I'm Louisa. *(She holds out her hand.)* At last!
(RUHELA doesn't take the offered hand.)

RUHELA You're a bit late.

LOUISA *(Still breathing heavily)* Tell me about it!

RUHELA I was just about/

LOUISA There was a problem, there was/

RUHELA I've a/

LOUISA In the subway, it was/

RUHELA I've a class to get to.

LOUISA A bomb scare, someone said it was a bomb scare.

RUHELA I'm sorry, but/

LOUISA We waited a half-hour for them to open the gates, but/

RUHELA I have/

LOUISA I'm not a brave soul so/

RUHELA I have a class/

LOUISA I hailed a cab.

RUHELA So I can't/

LOUISA The driver finally located this park...then a wheel dropped off of this darned thing and/

RUHELA I can't stay long.

LOUISA Honey, I'm sorry I kept you/

RUHELA So?

LOUISA As I said when I called, I just wished for us to/

RUHELA I can't miss my class, so/

LOUISA Sure, I understand, honey. And I have an airplane to catch very soon, and if there's any more trouble on the subway/

RUHELA *(Looks at her watch)* So...?

LOUISA And what with the three-hour check-ins we have to endure these days/

RUHELA I haven't got long.

LOUISA Yes honey, but I made this whole trip to see you, and I/

RUHELA I didn't invite you.

LOUISA I know, I know.

RUHELA Right.

LOUISA And it was foolish of me to arrive in your land without having made a proper arrangement. But...I so want us to talk a little and... I do have something for you. Something I want you to... *(She begins to open the travelling case.)*

RUHELA I don't want anything from you.

LOUISA Then... from Mel.

RUHELA Mel! I don't want anything from Mel!

LOUISA But I came all this way to/

RUHELA What made you think I'd want to see you?

LOUISA You gave me your mobile number, so you must have/

RUHELA I gave you my mobile number so you'd not phone the house again. I had to tell my father you were going to be teaching at my class. And I don't like telling lies. I never tell lies.

LOUISA And I am truly sorry if you had to tell a lie on my account, I/

RUHELA And I'm only here because you threatened to come to the house.

LOUISA That was not a threat. You just kept making arrangements then breaking them. Today was my last chance. I just needed to/

RUHELA So what do you *want?*

LOUISA I...

RUHELA *(Looking at her watch)* Yes? *(Looking at LOUISA) Yes?*

LOUISA Right now I'm not so sure. When I came here on that plane a week ago, it all seemed so simple.

RUHELA A total stranger turns up and/

LOUISA But we do share something/

RUHELA That was three years ago.

LOUISA Ruhela, there is this something I need to/

RUHELA It's 'Ruhella'. [Pronounces as Roo-hell-a]

LOUISA Excuse me. Ruhela. It may be three years, but you could so help me to/

RUHELA Help you? I don't know you. I never met you that time in New York. Then you turn up, out of the blue...

LOUISA I know, it was a dumb thing to do, but...

RUHELA Did you expect me to welcome you with open arms?

LOUISA Yeah, real dumb of me.

RUHELA So what's the reason?

LOUISA I have thought of you many times these past three years.

RUHELA Why?

LOUISA Well... your brother.

RUHELA Abs? What's Abs got to do with it, Abs is/

LOUISA Then I came across a card you gave to Mel.

RUHELA Abs! Mel! I don't want to/

LOUISA *(Has taken a postcard from her shoulder bag)* Here...

RUHELA *(Takes the card and reads)* 'Dear Mel. Guess who I've got the biggest crush on?'

LOUISA That's when I decided to be brave enough to come find you. When I finally had my airline ticket, I was about to make that call across the Atlantic. But I did not.

RUHELA Why not?

LOUISA Perhaps I feared you would not wish to see me. Well, I was proven right on that point, was I not? But I thought, go, just go. If she has moved, disappeared, then that is the will of the Lord. But you were there, on the end of that phone. And all I have been offered are excuses and put-offs, till this very last moment, when I am required to make my presence known in some run-down park, only to be informed that you have more pressing appointments. Well perhaps I shall just pick up this broken weight and head on home. *(She closes her travelling case.)* Indeed, I see now what a damn fool I have been, and that's the truth. To hope that a... conversation might take place. *(She starts to attempt to lift the case.)*

RUHELA What... sort of conversation?

LOUISA The conversation that I can never have with your brother.

(The attempts to lift the travelling case are defeating her. She breathes heavily and this turns into a fit of coughing. She taps her chest with her fist.

RUHELA takes a can of Coke from her bag. She opens it and offers it to LOUISA. She takes the Coke and drinks. The coughing subsides.) I thank you. *(A pause)*

RUHELA You alright?

LOUISA *(Taking breath)* Sure. Huh! 'Never purchase cheap luggage, it'll bust on you in the darnedest place', that's what my momma always said, and she's been proven right. I'll set myself down here awhile before I tackle that thing again. You go on to your... class, was it?

RUHELA Yeah.

LOUISA Class in what?

RUHELA Conducting.

LOUISA Con-what?

RUHELA *(Motions with her hand)* For an orchestra.

LOUISA So you're the musical type?

RUHELA I go to this evening class, once a week.

LOUISA Does it run in the family?

RUHELA What?

LOUISA Music. They say things run in a family. Mel sang in a rock and roll band at college. And Mel's daddy, he was the musical type.

RUHELA Saxophone.

LOUISA How did you know...? Why, yes...of course, Mel would have mentioned that. Not that tootin' on a saxophone is in the same league as conducting a whole orchestra. That's real classy. You gonna be a conductor one day? Standing up there, waving your arms at a whole battery of folk? You'd sure need some courage to do that.

RUHELA My mum doesn't like it.

LOUISA Why's that now?

RUHELA She says girls don't do that sort of thing.

LOUISA Girls should follow their star, same as boys.
RUHELA Dad's alright about it, he's a bit more modern.
LOUISA Then I'm with your daddy. Will you go to music college? After you done schooling?
RUHELA We couldn't afford it.
LOUISA Well then, perhaps I can/
RUHELA And anyway...
LOUISA Anyway what?
RUHELA I don't expect my husband would agree.
LOUISA Then you'll have chosen the wrong husband.
RUHELA 'Chosen!'
LOUISA Did I say something funny?
RUHELA You wouldn't understand.
LOUISA Anyways, you'll not be worrying about weddings awhile.
RUHELA If mum has her way I will.
LOUISA How come?
RUHELA She's saying next year.
LOUISA To get *married?*
RUHELA Dad says it can wait, but mum/
LOUISA How old are you?
RUHELA She's very traditional.
LOUISA Sixteen if you're a day.

The sound of thunder. They look up. The rustling of the leaves grows stronger.

RUHELA [In translation: No lightning, please God, no lightning.]
LOUISA You afraid of thunder, child?
RUHELA Lightning, I'm scared of the lightning, I...
LOUISA There's nothing to be afraid of, it's just God in a bad mood.

ABS has appeared. He is in his early twenties. He wears a smart business suit.

Thunder overhead. RUHELA screams.

LOUISA/ABS Hey, you're trembling like a newborn kitten.
RUHELA Don't let it come here.
LOUISA/ABS It won't, it won't come here, I promise.

Late summer 2001. New York.
A viewing platform, the World Trade Centre.

ABS Believe me.
RUHELA But Abs, we're so high up, it could...
ABS It's way out over New Jersey, over the water, see?
RUHELA It could change its mind and come here.
ABS It won't.
RUHELA This is the highest place in New York, you said so/
ABS We're safe as houses.
RUHELA Promise!
ABS For sure. There, there. Frightened of a bit of lightning? When you were brave enough to come all the way to America on your own?
RUHELA I didn't, I had to come with those horrible friends of dad's, and they/
ABS She's thirteen years old and she flies across the Atlantic without her family. That's real brave.
RUHELA You think?
ABS For sure.
RUHELA *(Mimicking an American accent)* 'For sure'.
ABS Okay, okay...
RUHELA *(Mimicking)* 'Real brave'. You're sounding *so* American.

The sound of thunder.

RUHELA [In translation: This is terrible!]

ABS It's fine, everything is fine.
RUHELA We're too high up.
ABS Your big brovs'll look out for you.
RUHELA How?
ABS Always did, always will.
RUHELA How can you *(Mimics an American accent)* 'look out for me'? When you live in New York and I/
ABS Ruhela. If you ever needed me, I'd be there. Just pick up the phone and I'll be on that plane.
RUHELA Wish you'd not come here, wish you'd never/
ABS Ah-hah! No wishing your life away... or mine...
RUHELA So why did you come here?
ABS Good job.
RUHELA You had a good job in London.
ABS And... other things...
RUHELA What other things?
ABS Well... once you've seen this town properly, you'll know. It's the only place to be. Look at it. *(Sings)* '...to be a part of it, New York, New York'. Come on, let's look over the edge.
RUHELA Oooh... nooo...
ABS You can't come to New York and not look over the edge of this bit of real estate. Come on. *(They are at the edge. They look down. ABS sings)* 'New York, New York, it's a wonderful town. The Bronx is up and the Battery's down...'

The sound of a plane getting nearer.

RUHELA How high up are we?
ABS Higher than anyone else in this city. In the world, maybe. These two towers are/
RUHELA *(Looks down)* The people... they're like insects. It's not natural.
ABS Not natural, eh?
RUHELA Building so high up, so/

ABS So tell me. Just how did you arrive in the land of the free this morning?
RUHELA Well...
ABS Exactly. So look up there. *(They look up.)* Now that plane is a good few thousand feet higher than these two 'scrapers. If you want 'unnatural', think about being in planes. Logic, little sister, logic.
RUHELA Yes, but in a plane it's...you can forget the height. Just watch the film or/
ABS 'Movie... movie'...you are in 'America'!
RUHELA There was this really nice American boy on the plane, my age and/
ABS Hey! Look out to the water.
RUHELA He was across the aisle from me and/
ABS See the lightning, dancing along the skyline.
RUHELA He was/
ABS Isn't that pretty?
RUHELA Abs! You're not listening to me!
ABS Sorry...so...?
RUHELA Anyway....
ABS There was this really nice boy?
RUHELA It doesn't matter.
ABS No. You met this really nice boy. So...
RUHELA What's the point?
ABS In really nice boys?
RUHELA Dad's friends said I shouldn't talk to strangers.
ABS Well sucks to them.
RUHELA They said/
ABS Hey! Did you get his email address?
RUHELA Why?
ABS You might have an American boyfriend!
RUHELA That's really stupid.
ABS You never know. And we say 'dumb', not 'stupid'.
RUHELA I don't care how it's said. Dad's friends are right and you don't understand.
ABS They're right to stop you talking to boys?

RUHELA When the time comes I'll still have to... have to get...

ABS You won't have to, not if you really don't want/

RUHELA Oh no? I can just hear mum. *(Mimics her mum)* [In translation: 'What'll the aunties back home in the village say about my wicked daughter?']

ABS You've never ever *been* to Bangladesh, let alone the village. You've never set eyes on the aunties, so who cares what they think!

RUHELA *(Mimicking the aunties)* 'That Ruhela in London, she's running wild, she's refusing her husband, she's bringing shame on the family.'

ABS Mum's a bit stuck in the past, she's/

RUHELA Even dad expects it.

ABS The world is changing Ruhela. Look at me. East End to the Big Apple.

RUHELA You're a boy.

ABS I'm a man of the world! Come on, I'm going to show you some more of New York. Then... we're having dinner with a friend.

RUHELA Who's that?

ABS Mel. And tomorrow we'll go to Coney Island and Brighton Beach.

RUHELA So this 'Mel'...?

ABS Yes?

RUHELA Is she... sort of...?

ABS Oh, no...Mel's/

RUHELA Your... *(Puts on an American accent)* 'sweetheart'.

ABS No, we/

RUHELA See, I'm becoming American too.

ABS I still go jogging and so does Mel. That's how we met and...and Mel's/

A roll of thunder. RUHELA screams.

RUHELA It's coming here, we're out in the open and it'll hit us!

ABS/LOUISA It's going somewhere else. There's nothing to be afraid of.

London. The present.
RUHELA covers her ears. LOUISA puts her arm around her.

LOUISA Believe me.
RUHELA I hate it!
LOUISA There... there...
RUHELA I'm always afraid that/
LOUISA When Mel was little and the lightning came, we'd huddle under the kitchen table. I used to say, 'Don't you worry, if the house comes tumbling down this old thing is made of good solid timber and we'll be safe and sound.'

Thunder, in the distance now.

LOUISA There now, it's passing over.
RUHELA I thought I'd grow out of it. But it's got worse, ever since... ever since...
LOUISA Sure, sure...I know, I know.
RUHELA It's stupid, to be afraid of/
LOUISA I used to say to Mel, it's okay to be scared. We've all got something that puts the frighteners on us. Mine's cockroaches. I can't abide those darned things. So... being afraid is not something to be ashamed of. You okay now?
RUHELA Yeah.
LOUISA See? We're still alive on God's good earth. Nothing to fear.

Pause

RUHELA I... I was afraid to meet you.
LOUISA Afraid of *me?* Of one old gal?
RUHELA I made my mind up this wouldn't happen.

LOUISA That much is clear. But here we are. *(A silence. The leaves rustle in the trees. There is the sound of a plane or a helicopter in the sky. RUHELA looks up.)* Why 'afraid'?
RUHELA I can go whole days and not think about Abs. Sometimes a whole week. Then I'll hear mum calling his name in her sleep. But I only feel... feel...
LOUISA Feel...?
RUHELA What does hate feel like?
LOUISA You hate him? Surely not...
RUHELA Something like... like...
LOUISA Your own brother? Even after/
RUHELA You wouldn't understand.
LOUISA Try me.
RUHELA He brought shame on himself... on our family.
LOUISA Ah!
RUHELA You know what I mean?
LOUISA Maybe I do.
RUHELA So...
LOUISA Well... your brother did not give rise to feelings of 'love' in my heart...
RUHELA So when you met him...?
LOUISA I refused to meet him.
RUHELA But you still felt/
LOUISA I guess I hated the *idea* of him. Yeah. But if I *had* met him...
RUHELA What then?
LOUISA It is a very easy thing, to hate someone you have never met. That is the easiest thing in the world. And it feels so... comfortable. So... righteous.
RUHELA I wish...
LOUISA You wish?

Pause

RUHELA I hate America.
LOUISA Yeah, I have heard variations on that theme this past week. America... the fount of all that is

wrong in this world today. But... *(She indicates the Coke can and the McDonald's carton.)* ...oh my, you all sure do love to grab our goodies.

MEL has appeared. He is a young white man in his early twenties. He wears casual clothes. He has a large tub of popcorn. RUHELA loosens her hijab.

LOUISA/MEL Now that's truly pretty hair you have, young lady.

New York. Coney Island.
Sounds of a funfair. Hurdy-gurdy funfair music in the distance, mixed in with tannoy-music. Frank Sinatra singing: 'Fly Me to the Moon'. MEL has been listening to it. RUHELA is writing postcards.

MEL Yes sir, real pretty.
RUHELA Thanks Mel.
MEL Some Coney Island popcorn?
RUHELA Please.
MEL It's a real shame to keep it covered up. *(Holds out the popcorn)* There you go, princess.
RUHELA It's our custom.
MEL Eh?
RUHELA For the women to cover their heads.
MEL Why?
RUHELA Modesty.
MEL Okay, each to his own. Now where's that brother of yours?
RUHELA He's still trying to win a fluffy dog.
MEL *(Calls and waves)* Hey big spender, call it a day! We're going down the beach!
RUHELA (*Calls)* If you win I want the blue one!
MEL *(Picks up a postcard)* Writing home?
RUHELA I promised dad a picture of the Statue of Liberty.
MEL You love your poppa?

RUHELA 'Course. D'you love yours?
MEL Dead.
RUHELA That's sad.
MEL Hear that song? He used to play that tune for me on his saxophone. When I was just little.

He listens for a moment. RUHELA watches him.

RUHELA Mel?
MEL Yeah?
RUHELA Is it Coney Island with a 'K' or a 'C'?
MEL A 'C'.
RUHELA *(Reads)* 'We've come to a great place with Abs' best friend, Mel. It's got rides and games, and it's called...'*(Writes)* 'Coney Island'. That's for my best friend, Towhida.
MEL You got places like Coney and Brighton Beach in the UK?
RUHELA Lots. And one of them is called Brighton, too. Only it's got stones, not sand. We go down there in the summer with all the neighbours. Mum makes a big picnic and we sit on blankets in a big circle and eat. Then we paddle and look for seashells.
MEL Sounds fun.
RUHELA Mum sits there all covered up, but dad doesn't mind if I show my head.
MEL So... what is it... with this scarf thing?
RUHELA Hijab. It's called the hijab.
MEL 'Hijab'. Okay. But isn't it bothersome? I mean... *(RUHELA laughs)* Hey now, what have I said?
RUHELA 'Bothersome'.
MEL It's a decent word.
RUHELA It's like...well, it's English, but it sounds... *foreign*. Like last night, when we came for dinner...
MEL Only it was 'supper'...
RUHELA And you said 'the restroom's down there...'
MEL And you thought *I* thought you were tired...

RUHELA When I just wanted a pee. And the flat was an 'apartment', and the sofa was a 'couch'...

MEL Yeah, yeah...and don't go hogging the popcorn, little lady.

RUHELA And the underground's 'the subway'...

MEL And I could've said, you'll find the 'john' in the 'lobby' instead of... what is it?

RUHELA *(Putting on a very 'Queen's English' voice)* 'The toilet is in the hallway.'

MEL Now that's *real* weird.

RUHELA Not as weird as American.

MEL But... don't you go to the movies? That's how we speak on the movies.

RUHELA But this is real life and it sounds/

MEL Princess, the movies *are* real life, only bigger and better. D'you go to the movies?

RUHELA I saw *Titanic* three times and we've got it on DVD.

MEL You ever seen *King Kong?*

RUHELA Who's King Kong?

MEL He's a great big giant ape. And he carries this girl to the top of the World Trade Centre. That's the colour version. In the black-and-white one it was the Empire State, but in the colour it's one of them twins. Right up it with that girl in the palm of his hand.

RUHELA What for?

MEL 'Cause he's in love with her.

RUHELA Ugh!

MEL No, he goes 'ugh'! *(He puts his arm around RUHELA and beats his chest with the other.)* Uggauggauggauggah!

RUHELA Mel! People are watching.

Pause

MEL Then they kill him.

RUHELA That's sad.

MEL He's on top of that twin tower, with the girl, and they fly planes at him and they kill him. Always makes me cry, just thinking of it...

RUHELA Oh, Mel...

MEL What a chump I am. When I played it for Abs and it got to the end and I cried, he laughed at me. Well, I guess I'm a sentimental chump. Hey! I'm a big chump for a big chimp! *(A pause)* He really did love the girl.

Pause

RUHELA I'm glad you're not a girl.

MEL Eh?

RUHELA When Abs said 'Mel' I thought it was a girl's name. Like short for Melanie or something. I thought I'd have to sit there all evening with him making soppy faces at you. Yuk!

MEL Right.

RUHELA So, when we get to the beach, shall we paddle in the sea?

MEL If you like.

RUHELA That's another weird thing about here.

MEL Well, I guess we're pretty darned weird altogether.

RUHELA New York having a beach. *(Calls)* Abs! We're going to have a paddle!

MEL So do they let you take your shoes and socks off?

RUHELA Who?

MEL Your... people. In your... religion? *(RUHELA does not reply.)* Joke? *(RUHELA does not reply.)* Not so funny, eh?

RUHELA It's okay.

MEL I'm sorry.

Pause

RUHELA I wasn't *really* laughing at you back then.

MEL Of that I am aware.
RUHELA That's it!
MEL Excuse me?
RUHELA And that!
MEL I'm lost...
RUHELA *That's* what I like about real-life American when you speak it. It's sort of... old fashioned. And... polite.
MEL I got that from my momma. *(Puts on a southern drawl)* She grew up in the state of Mississippi, and the folk down there are exceedingly gracious in their speech.
RUHELA *(Collecting up her postcards)* All done.
MEL *(Picks up the card he had looked at before)* Don't forget this one.
RUHELA That's for you.
MEL I can get one any time.
RUHELA Look on the back.
MEL *(He turns the card over and reads)* 'Guess who I've got the *biggest crush* on?' Well now, who could that be, I wonder?
RUHELA Not telling.
MEL Well he'll be one happy guy. You got the American way of saying it down real neat.
RUHELA Did I get it right?
MEL '... the biggest crush'. Yeah, that's real American.
RUHELA It's got my address, too. So you can write to me. The email address is there too, but I like to get proper letters as well.
MEL *(In a southern drawl)* I will surely be penning ya'all my fond words of greeting.
RUHELA And there's our phone number, so you can call me.
MEL Right y'are, ma'am.

ABS enters. He is wearing casual clothes. He is carrying a large, fluffy bright green starfish.

ABS They'd run out of dogs.
RUHELA What *is* it?
ABS It's a starfish.
MEL It's gross!
RUHELA There's no such thing as a fluffy green starfish!
ABS You wanted a fluffy blue dog!
MEL Okay, let's take it to the beach. Maybe we'll find a real starfish and they can fall in love.
RUHELA Starfish can't fall in love.
MEL Who're you to say who can't fall in love?
RUHELA Men and women fall in love.
MEL Starfish men and starfish women!
ABS Not if they have arranged marriages.
RUHELA Shut up Abs!
ABS Then they just do what the starfish parents say.
RUHELA I said/
MEL Now just what...
RUHELA He's just being stupid.
ABS [In translation: Just telling the truth.]
RUHELA [In translation: I hate you!]
MEL *(To ABS)* Just what's going on here?
RUHELA/ABS You wouldn't understand.
MEL/LOUISA Well try me, just try me.

London. The present.
The sound of fire engines in the distance.

LOUISA If you want to. I'd like to understand.

RUHELA is fastening her hijab.

RUHELA I'll be late for my class.
LOUISA Yeah, I guess.
RUHELA And you've your plane.
LOUISA Sure.

RUHELA So...
LOUISA So...?
RUHELA Did you love your husband?
LOUISA Mister saxophone?
RUHELA Did you?
LOUISA Oh sure, I was like a rabbit in the headlights. But he played in bands, see. All over the state of Mississippi. Pretty soon I had news coming back to me 'bout all them little ladies hangin' round the bandstand. Then his whisky-habit made itself known and next thing I knew I'd be getting a slap if I opened my mouth. I kept all that from Mel. He adored his daddy, did Mel. Liked to hear his daddy play that saxophone for him. But there came a time when I was fearing for my life, so that's when I took Mel and me up to New York. Mel was 'bout five year old at the time. I told him his daddy had died.
RUHELA That's... that's...
LOUISA And that's God's truth, and may God strike me down for it. But sometimes a lie is better than the truth. And that's the truth about love, from where I stand.
RUHELA I think my mum loves my dad.
LOUISA Yeah?
RUHELA Well... they never fight. I mean, mum shouts a bit when things go wrong in the house. Or when he lets me do things she doesn't approve of...
LOUISA Like learning to be a conductor?
RUHELA But he just winks and grins and the storm blows over. And sometimes I hear them giggling at night. In the bedroom, so...
LOUISA Well I am glad for that.
RUHELA It's a bit yuk... at their age.
LOUISA Were they childhood sweethearts?
RUHELA 'Course not.
LOUISA Some folk are.
RUHELA Not if it's arranged.
LOUISA Oh sure, sure... yeah... your way, of course. Well, maybe that has its merits. Sure wish I'd been 'arranged', if it turns out as giggling in the bedroom.

There sure weren't much of that in my wedded life. *(Pause)* So this man you're getting hitched to...?

RUHELA Betrothed.
LOUISA Ah-hah. He lives in London?
RUHELA He's in Bangladesh.
LOUISA But you have met him?
RUHELA No.
LOUISA Well, I'll be!
RUHELA I like his photograph. He looks quite... sweet. I think.
LOUISA You... think?
RUHELA I... think so.
LOUISA But what do you feel?
RUHELA Feel?
LOUISA Feel.

MEL has appeared.

RUHELA/MEL What do I feel for him?

New York, 2001. Central Park.

LOUISA Yeah. I want to know what you feel for him.

A gust of wind and the sounds of leaves blowing.

MEL Alright... I... feel/
LOUISA No, no don't tell me.
MEL Well, do you wanna know or not?
LOUISA This is something that happens to other folks.
MEL This is the twenty-first century!
LOUISA This is something that... and why did you have to bring me to Central Park to tell me?
MEL I just thought/
LOUISA Why couldn't you have dropped the bomb in my own home?

MEL Because I reckoned if we were in a public place, there'd be less chance of you hollerin' and bawlin'. So calm down mom, just...
LOUISA Okay, okay... I'm calm... I'm real calm.
MEL Good.
LOUISA Jesus, I could do with a cigarette...
MEL You know what the doctor said, mom...
LOUISA Yeah, yeah but... okay, okay. So.
MEL So?
LOUISA So... I'm calm, right?
MEL Right.
LOUISA So my son is a homo/
MEL Mom!
LOUISA Sorry, sorry.
MEL Okay.
LOUISA My son is... a *gay*.
MEL 'Gay', mom. Not 'a' gay. I'm not a darned *thing*.
LOUISA Well... however it's put, it just don't seem right, it/
MEL Mom, we've been over and over this/
LOUISA I mean the word. The word don't seem right. Lord, I must have a smoke, I surely must/
MEL Please mom...
LOUISA *(Looks in her bag)* I'm sure there was a pack in here...
MEL Go ahead, go ahead and kill yourself!
LOUISA If anything's killing me – it's you. Telling me that you're... no, I just can't say it.
MEL Mom, words don't kill.
LOUISA You grow up with a word and the word seems... fitting. Homo. Then along come a bunch of folk making their demands, and the word's wiped clean off the map. And Lord save the sinner that let's the word slip out.
MEL I ain't heard you saying 'nigger' for many a year, mom.
LOUISA Well, that's different.
MEL How – different?

LOUISA There was a case there. They deserve some respect and I can see that, I/

MEL And I don't? I don't deserve some respect for who I am?

LOUISA But 'gay'? 'Gay'! It sounds like... a frock I wore at a pre-teen party. Something pink with frills on. Lord save me, you're still a man, and... well... 'homo' at least has got a manly sort'a ring to it.

MEL 'Manly', eh? *(Adopts a deep mock-cowboy drawl and posture)* 'Hey pard'ner, let's saddle up them hosses and hit that good ol' trail down to Wy-o-ming an' have us a real good hoe-down with a bunch'a ho-mos'.

LOUISA You just ain't gonna take me seriously are you?

MEL Mom, *you* are refusing to take *me* seriously.

LOUISA I'm in a state of shock. *(Takes out a packet of cigarettes from her bag)* I'll only have one, I promise.

MEL It's your life.

LOUISA And what about *your* life?

MEL I want to live it in the light.

LOUISA And I want you to live. But there's folk out there in this world... folk who wish to do serious harm to/

MEL Mom, this is New York. This is the year two thousand and one. We are living in the modern age. This city is full of gay people and no one gives a damn. We'll have gay marriages soon. We're everywhere and/

LOUISA But you're a fire-fighter! You're in the New York City Fire Department!

MEL So?

LOUISA Quit laughing at me.

MEL You are being ridiculous.

LOUISA The two things just don't go together.

MEL Being gay and fighting fires?

LOUISA *(Looking in her bag)* Now where is that lighter...?

MEL *(Takes the packet of cigarettes from her)* No, mom.
LOUISA And here is something else, my boy – it's against God.
MEL Now that is taking it too far.
LOUISA I know my bible.
MEL Jesus hung out with twelve guys!
LOUISA And I have a line son, a *line* when it comes to what is right and what is wrong.
MEL Mom!
LOUISA I know, I know. I've not always been little miss goody-two-shoes, I/
MEL Too darn right. How many saxophone players did I have to call 'uncle'?
LOUISA Yeah, well... And if you're going to do this gay thing, you just keep away from saxophone players – they're nothing but trouble. So go on, tell me. Who is he and what does he do?
MEL He's a systems analyst and his name is Abs. I... have a photograph of him... *(Takes it out of his pocket)*
LOUISA And what is a 'systems analyst', pray? *(She has found the lighter.)* And hand me back those cigarettes.
MEL *(Teasing her with the cigarettes)* He works in the World Trade Centre... top of one 'a them little towers... he's a real man of business.
LOUISA *(Grabbing for the cigarettes)* Give me those...
MEL And his little sister is in town – she's real cute.
LOUISA Now just you give those here...
MEL So I thought, how 'bout we take them to a Broadway show? Abs is crazy about musicals and I have these tickets for/
LOUISA Abs?
MEL Yeah, Abs – his name is Abs.
LOUISA Now what sort of a name is that?
MEL *(Looking at the photograph)* It's... just his/
LOUISA Hey now! Abs? It sounds sort'a... He's not Jewish, is he?
MEL Ah... no, mom.

LOUISA Because I have nothing against them, as a race. But I do not believe in mixing. I will, with great seriousness, accept you for what you are. Because I love you and I do not want to lose you. But I was raised with some notions and I have my lines, and I cannot, nor will not abandon them because/

MEL Mom. Abs is not Jewish.

LOUISA Right. So... the photograph... *(She holds out her hand. MEL hesitates.)* Come on, son. I'm ready to move on.

He hands the photograph over. She takes the photograph. She looks at it for a moment. Then she hands it back.

ABS has entered.

MEL/ABS Don't cry. Please don't cry. I hate it when you cry.

LOUISA walks away.

New York, 2001. Outside a theatre on Broadway. RUHELA has loosened her hijab.

ABS I just hate it. *(Holds out a handkerchief to Ruhela)* Here, mop those up. Now what brought this on? One minute we're walking down Broadway like we've got the world at our feet, the next you're sobbing your heart out.

RUHELA I'm sorry, I just...

ABS We can't have tears on your last night in the Big Apple.

RUHELA I know.

ABS Mel won't want to see you blubbing.

RUHELA I know.

ABS This is our big treat of the week. He must've paid a fortune for the tickets.

RUHELA I know.

ABS And what'll his mum think?
RUHELA I know.
ABS Okay?
RUHELA Yeah.
ABS Good. So... we're on Broadway. Look at it, isn't this just the place to be? We're going to see a real Broadway show and then/
RUHELA And then I'll get on the plane and... and...
ABS Is this what the tears were about, eh? Ruhela, you can come again. Any time you want, I'll fly you out, just give the word.
RUHELA I hate those friends of father's.
ABS Next time I'll come over and get you... come on, sis, you're being silly.
RUHELA They're...
ABS They've been very kind.
RUHELA They're so...
ABS They organised their whole vacation so they could fly with you. Good – blow, now.
RUHELA *(Blowing her nose)* There you go. 'Vacation'. It's a 'holiday', in case you'd forgotten. Anyway, they're... boring.
ABS Watch the film.
RUHELA They made me turn the film off on the way here. They said it was 'unsuitable' for a Muslim.
ABS Well... it's only a few hours. You've the rest of your life after that.
RUHELA That's just it!
ABS What?
RUHELA The rest of my life.
ABS [In translation: So that's it.]
RUHELA It all seems so... small. So... sort of...
ABS Planned?
RUHELA I wish you could come back with me.
ABS My life's here.
RUHELA Why?
ABS I can... breathe... here.
RUHELA I don't understand.
ABS You will... one day.

MEL has entered. He stands and looks at them.

ABS Ruhela. I think you are a very good... and... dutiful... daughter to our parents. I think you wish to do what is right, and I salute you for that. But you have your own individual life to... *(He sees MEL.)* Hey! About time...

MEL Abs. Hi, princess.

RUHELA Hi Mel. Where's your mum?

MEL She... couldn't make it.

ABS Anything wrong?

MEL No problems.

ABS There's a problem.

MEL Okay, there's a problem.

ABS I know that face.

MEL *(Holds out a glossy theatre programme)* Princess, here's the programme for the show. How 'bout you read up on the story. You can give me and Abs the low-down.

She takes the programme. MEL draws ABS to one side.

ABS So...?

MEL Let's just leave it.

ABS Tell me.

MEL Not here, not/

ABS We don't have secrets, we/

MEL Okay, you want to know?

ABS Yes.

MEL I told her.

ABS Told her what?

MEL What d'you think?

ABS Us?

MEL So, let's go see the show.

ABS How did she take it?

MEL She's not here, is she?

ABS Well... maybe it was... bad timing.

MEL Bad timing! I've lost my mother and all you can say is 'bad timing'!

ABS I didn't mean/
MEL Easy for you.
ABS Meaning?
MEL At least I stood my ground like a man and told her.
ABS Look, you did a brave thing, but/
MEL At least I didn't run away!
ABS Mel, don't. We never fight, we never/
RUHELA *(Calls over)* Can we go in?
ABS In a minute, Mel and I have/
RUHELA It's nearly time.
ABS I said *in a minute!*
MEL I've lost her. Because of... because of...
ABS Me? Us?
MEL She's the only one I'll ever have.
ABS Okay, it was really brave of you and it didn't work out, but she'll/
MEL You don't know her. Dumb, I'm just plain dumb. Thinking she'd take it all on board. Thinking we'd all go out on the town, one big happy family, everything out in the open.

RUHELA crosses towards them.

ABS And did you think about me, about what/
MEL Right! That would have been a real big problem for you, eh?
ABS I mean/
MEL 'We won't tell her, she's too young.'
RUHELA What am I too young for?
ABS It's more than that/
MEL What then?
ABS It's our faith, it's/
MEL Your faith!
ABS Yes, my/
MEL Since when did I ever hear you mention your/
RUHELA Please stop it...
ABS You don't understand/

MEL You're a coward.
RUHELA Stop it! Stop it! *(A pause)* You mustn't. You mustn't fight. You love each other.
ABS Yes. We do. That's what this is all about. Mel and me. We love each other.
ABS/MEL/RUHELA/LOUISA We love each other.

London. The present.
The sound of fire-engines and police sirens in the distance.

LOUISA That's what he said. 'Mom, I have met a man and we love each other.' The truth, plain and simple. And I shut my heart down. Well now...
(She turns towards her case. RUHELA puts her ear-phones on. She listens to her CD. LOUISA does not notice this and she starts to open her case.)
You have your class and I have my plane, so I'm hoping you will now accept what I have here. Now let me see... *(She takes out a few items of clothing.)*
That's another thing my momma said. 'Travel light, girl, wherever you go in life.' Never heeded her, did I? Oh no, I'll have me an overnight stay somewhere and I'll throw in enough undergarments for a six month siege. *(She holds up an item of clothing that is particularly garish.)* Now what did I bring this along for? 'Specting to meet the Queen of England at Buckingham Palace, was I?
(She turns and holds out the garment to RUHELA. RUHELA is still listening to her CD. She motions with her finger in time with the music.)
Hey! Anyone there? *(RUHELA removes her earphones.)* Have I been talking to myself?
RUHELA Sorry.
LOUISA No matter. *(Holds up the garment)* So what is your opinion of this little item?
RUHELA It's... it's...
LOUISA Ridiculous, yeah...
RUHELA No, it's...

LOUISA Don't you worry, even I know that. I look in the mirror some days and all I see is that old hunk'a mutton dressed up like a spring lamb.
RUHELA No, you're not really...
LOUISA So what have you been listening to?
RUHELA Oh, nothing...
LOUISA Been swinging that finger in time to nothing?
RUHELA It's... classical... it's not...
LOUISA Not what?
RUHELA Just...
LOUISA Not for the likes of me? *(She takes the earphones. Listens)* Why that is just... *(She hums along for a moment.)* I have not heard this for many a year. *(She removes the earphones.)*
RUHELA You know it?
LOUISA Doo-vor-zhack? Sure. *(RUHELA laughs)* Is that so funny?
RUHELA The way you say it. *(Mimics)* 'Doo-vor-zhack'.
LOUISA Well... however it's said...
RUHELA D'you really know it?
LOUISA Honey, just 'cause I'm white trash...
RUHELA I didn't mean...
LOUISA White trash is what I am... but that does not mean I've had a life that's been totally devoid of things cultural. We were dirt poor, but my daddy had a record collection. Beethoven, Tchaikovsky, you name 'em he had 'em. An' I especially loved this *(She exaggerates her own accent.)* 'Doo-vor-zhack'. This here is the New World Symphony. So don't you go thinking I'm just made up of flashy clothes. *(She listens again.)* This here's my favourite part. Here... *(She hands one of the earphones to RUHELA. RUHELA loosens her hijab. With one each of the earphones they listen together, humming along. LOUISA copies RUHELA'S gestures. Then she suddenly removes her earphone.)*
RUHELA What's the matter?
LOUISA It brought my daddy back.

RUHELA Does that make you sad?

LOUISA Yeah, but... now I'm thinking how Mel had no proper daddy of his own, and... Honey, d'you think that's the reason?

RUHELA Reason for what?

LOUISA For a boy to turn out as gay? D'you think having a good, strong father, someone to look up to and respect, would stop that happening?

RUHELA Well...

LOUISA There has to be a *reason*.

RUHELA Abs hero-worshipped our dad, when he was little. It still happened to him.

LOUISA It sits on me heavy, sometimes.

RUHELA What does?

LOUISA That lie I told, 'bout his daddy being dead. Perhaps the man has changed. People do change, don't they? From the bad to the good.

RUHELA Or the other way round.

LOUISA Oh, I do pray for my boy. Each night before I sleep, I say a prayer for him.

RUHELA Does it work?

LOUISA Don't you have prayer?

RUHELA Of course we do.

LOUISA And you send the words out into the universe. Little birds of hope, flying away, to perform their tasks.

RUHELA Words are invisible.

LOUISA So is the soul but it is there.

RUHELA But words... you say them and they've gone.

LOUISA It's my notion they don't. It's my notion they're still out there. Like the very words we are speaking, right this very moment.

RUHELA But, even if they are out there, we'll never know.

LOUISA There's a machine that records mister 'Doo-vor-zhak's' symphony, right? Captures it and puts it on a disc, so we can play it back?

RUHELA Ye...es.

LOUISA And I'll lay bets, one day there'll be a machine that can capture every single thing that's ever been spoke or sung. Bring them back. How 'bout that? We'll all be on playback.

RUHELA It'll never happen.

LOUISA Maybe not... but we fly across God's blue sky in planes, don't we? We walk on the moon. We build ourselves towers that scrape the heavens. So why not a machine that can bring back every word that has ever been uttered? When we will know everything that has passed.

RUHELA Only God knows everything.

LOUISA Sure. And that's why I pray. I've let fly more bad words in my life than you could shake a stick at. So when I pray, I'm sending some good words after 'em. I hope that when I die, the good will outweigh the bad.

MEL has entered.
London/New York.

RUHELA/MEL *(To LOUISA)* I don't know what to do. I don't know how to make it better.

MEL Don't make me choose between you and him, Mom. Don't draw a line between us. Just meet him. You might not like him, but it'll be *him* you're not caring for, not the colour of his skin. Give him... me, you... us... a chance. Mom, you have always taught me to do the good thing. Now do a good thing for me. Just say the good word. Just say 'yes'. Mom. Please.

ABS has entered.

LOUISA/ABS *(To RUHELA)* I want to make it better for you. With all my heart, I do.

ABS But I can't find the words, little sister. Or you won't hear the words. When you met Mel you liked him, you really liked him. I was even a bit jealous. Don't get on the plane like this. Remember what mum always said when anyone had a row at home? She said, 'Never go to sleep at night on a quarrel.' She made us make friends again before we went to bed... herself included ... and that was saying something. Well, I'm saying, never get on a plane on a quarrel. Ruhela, please don't go through those gates without saying we're friends. Ruhela. Please.

London.
The sound of fire engines and police cars.

LOUISA There's something going on out there. Still, we must be brave. We must not let them get the upper hand.
RUHELA 'Them'?
LOUISA Well... whoever 'they' are. Now. I want to give you something.
RUHELA Well... I...
LOUISA My momma said/ *(RUHELA laughs)* I know, I know, I'm always saying what my momma said to do/
RUHELA And you never remember to do it!
LOUISA She said, 'Learning to receive graciously is just as important as learning to give generously.' There we have it. *(She takes out a large, thick envelope from the case.)* That is what you must receive from me. *(RUHELA takes the envelope.)* Go on. *(RUHELA opens the envelope. She looks inside.)*
It's yours.
RUHELA I... I can't.
LOUISA Remember what my momma said.
RUHELA But...
LOUISA *(Putting things back in her case)* Well... I'd better think about that flight. And you'd better think about that class.
RUHELA *(Holding up the envelope)* Is this what you came here for?
LOUISA Well, not just/
RUHELA You said it was from Mel.
LOUISA It kind'a is, but/

RUHELA What's he trying to do, is he/
LOUISA Mel can't do anything, he's/
RUHELA Just tell him/
LOUISA I can't tell my son anything.
RUHELA Well I'm telling you, I don't want this... *(She pulls out a thick pile of paper money from the envelope.)* You can tell him/
LOUISA How can I tell him?
RUHELA With words. Just say, 'Ruhela hates America. America stole her brother and brought shame on her family. Ruhela does not need your money for her dowry.' Tell him that.
LOUISA I cannot tell him that.
RUHELA Why not?
LOUISA Of course... how would you know?

MEL has entered. He has his fire-fighter's jacket slung over his shoulder. ABS has entered. He has his business suit on and carries a briefcase.

The sound of fire engines and police cars.

London/New York, September 10, 2001.
Telephone Conversations.
(No need for actual phones, except where indicated.)

ABS Ruhela. It's Abs here. Dad said you got back safely, but I wanted to know from you that everything was alright. Ruhela...?
RUHELA Yes
ABS The journey... was it okay?
RUHELA Yes.
ABS And did you... meet any nice boys?
RUHELA No.
ABS And dad's friends... were they okay with you?
RUHELA No.

ABS Did you tell mum and dad all about the visit? *(A silence)* All the things we did? *(A silence)* Ruhela...? Did you tell them... all about it?

RUHELA Don't worry, your secret is safe with me.

ABS I didn't mean/

RUHELA And don't bother to phone again, ever. You're not my brother any more. You have brought shame on us all. So stay in America, live/

ABS I can't live anywhere if you don't love me.

RUHELA As far as I'm concerned, you're dead.

ABS Ruhela... Ruhela...

MEL *(On mobile)* Abs, it's Mel. Did you get my previous message? I have the day off tomorrow, is there any chance you could take a day out, as well? I think we need some time together. You could come and stay over at my place tonight. I'll cook us a great meal, we could put on a movie. How 'bout *West Side Story?* I promise I won't cry when it gets to the sad ending. Then tomorrow we can drive someplace upstate. See some open space, walk in the trees. The weather folk promise us a clear blue September sky tomorrow.

ABS Hi, Mel. Got all your messages, sorry I didn't get back. Now your line's engaged, so I'll text as well. Not sure about tomorrow, we've some new clients coming on board and they're big. I've a lot of paper-work to get through tonight, and I'll probably need to be at my desk first thing. The blue sky sounds nice, though... but...

LOUISA Son, I've been thinking...

MEL *(On mobile)* Mom, if this is going to be another set-to...

LOUISA No, no, don't hang up. I'm not about to shoot my mouth off again. It's just that... I've been thinking about your father...

MEL 'Bout poppa? Now why, after all these years, should you be/

LOUISA I've been turning some things over in my mind.
MEL What sort'a things?
LOUISA Well... I've never been exactly truthful about him, you see. To you, I mean. There is something... something...
MEL Like...?
LOUISA I'd rather not say on the phone. You said you had a day off work tomorrow?
MEL Ye...es.
LOUISA Why don't you come around? I could make your favourite/
MEL Tomorrow could be difficult...
LOUISA Tonight even...
MEL I'll have to get back to you. I'm, still on duty and the guys are waving at me.
LOUISA You take care now...
MEL It'll be kids trashing something and making bonfires.

ABS Mel, how about this? Tomorrow's meeting has been rescheduled for the morning. There's nothing in my diary for the afternoon. So I'll jump ship at lunchtime and we can hit the road. Blue skies, hey?

MEL *(On mobile)* I guess you've gone to bed, mom. Sorry I didn't get back to you this evening. Some kids trashing a store in Lower East Side. We caught the blaze before the lot went up. I will be round tomorrow morning. I have to leave by lunch, but I'm hoping that will give us some time to talk about poppa. And... I'm going to be honest here... I am leaving at lunch so's I can spend the rest of the day with Abs. And momma... I'm going to spend the rest of my life with him. Hear that? My life.

LOUISA I've just woken up in the night, son, and I got your message. It made me real happy to know that I'll see you tomorrow morning... no, this morning, it's well gone midnight. I dug out some old photographs of you and your daddy, him playing on that old saxophone and you smiling away like you was in heaven. I'm going back to my bed now. I'll lay me down and pray for us all.

A sound in the distance. It could be a plane. It continues throughout the following sequence, getting nearer and nearer. RUHELA, LOUISA, ABS and MEL all look up. The following lines are on the sound-system, interspersed with the approaching sound.

We'll all be on playback.
Only God knows everything.
The weather folk promise us a clear blue September sky.
Please don't go through those gates without saying we're friends.
I have nothing against them as a race. But I do not believe in mixing.
It's not natural.
It's a very easy thing, to hate someone you have never met.
Jesus hung out with twelve guys.
Starfish can't fall in love.
Hey! I'm a big chump for a big chimp!
Guess who I've got the biggest crush on
And I shut my heart down.
I'm glad you're not a girl.
He's on top of that tower, with the girl, and they fly planes at him and kill him.
There's nothing to be afraid of, it's just God in a bad mood.
Your big brovs'll look out for you.
I want to live in the light.
And there's something else, my boy, it's against God.
As far as I'm concerned, you're dead.

The approaching sound has fully arrived. It is the sound of a plane impacting on a building.

Silence.

London. The present.

LOUISA He never did come round to see me that morning, of course. All those fire-fighting boys had no day off, that day.

Pause

RUHELA When it happened, there was a picture in all the papers... one of the firemen...
LOUISA The boy climbing the stairwell?
RUHELA He looked a bit like...
LOUISA He made it, you know.
RUHELA Mel? Mel made it?
LOUISA No. The guy in the papers. He came back down. I met him. Some ceremony for the families. He knew Mel. He said Mel was ahead of him, in that stairwell, going up those stairs, in that tower...

Pause

RUHELA I thought it was *King Kong*.
LOUISA King Kong?
RUHELA The film. I was sitting in a coffee bar in Aldgate. That morning. With my dad. There was a little television on. But not the sound. The tower burst into flames. I thought they'd just got the big ape. With the girl in his hand. That's what I thought. When I saw it.

Pause

LOUISA The big ape! Oh my, I shouldn't be laughing, but... *(Her laugh turns into a cough. She picks up the can of Coke from the ground and drinks. Her breathing subsides.)*

RUHELA You alright?

LOUISA For now. That's better. Wanna know something else my momma said? She said, 'There's one thing you can bet on in this life... you'll have tears at a wedding and laughter at a funeral.' You thought it was a film about an ape. Oh my.

RUHELA I'm sorry about Mel.

LOUISA I know. *(She puts the Coke can back on the ground. The McDonald's carton lies there too. She looks at them and at the other items of litter.)* I have never in all my born days seen so much trash on the ground since I came to this country of yours. *(Looks at her watch)* Well, time's come. And honey... I have to tell you something. Before I'm gone.

RUHELA Yes?

LOUISA When I saw the pictures on the screen, while they were telling us what had just happened...

RUHELA You don't have to say...

LOUISA When I turned on the TV that morning and saw those pictures – for a moment – just that one small moment... I was glad.

RUHELA I don't understand.

LOUISA They say those men were evil. But whatever 'evil' is, some tiny part of it must lurk in my heart. For in that moment... I rejoiced.

RUHELA But... your son died.

LOUISA In that moment, in my mind, he was still coming round to see me. He had told me he would not be at work that day, so/

RUHELA And you knew that Abs was in that/

LOUISA Just for a moment, but have you/

RUHELA You hoped/

LOUISA Never/

RUHELA That he/

LOUISA Wished/

RUHELA Was/

LOUISA Someone/
RUHELA/LOUISA Dead?
(RUHELA looks at the money. She holds it out to LOUISA.)
LOUISA That is what they paid me, for his life. *(RUHELA continues to hold it out.)* It burns a hole in my pocket. *(RUHELA continues to hold it out.)* You could go to college.
RUHELA Live off his blood?
LOUISA You could be free to/
RUHELA Those cowards killed him and/
LOUISA Not cowards/
RUHELA You wished him dead. You're no better/
LOUISA They were/
RUHELA Than those/
LOUISA Not/
RUHELA/LOUISA Cowards. *(A silence)*
LOUISA Not cowards. A terrible thing they did. A very wrong thing. But not cowards.
RUHELA How can you say that?
LOUISA They were brave men.
RUHELA Evil!
LOUISA They believed what they were doing was right. And a coward does not fly himself into a building.
RUHELA And now my father gets spit in his face on the street. We are called terrorists. *(She tightens her hijab.)* A piece of cloth on my head is seen as a flag of war.
LOUISA And that is wrong. And that moment of rejoicing in my heart, that was wrong. But in that moment I was no better, no worse, than those men flying that plane towards your brother.
RUHELA They should be/
LOUISA And I want no revenge, I/
RUHELA They should/
LOUISA No revenge in my heart, or taken on my behalf.
RUHELA But don't you feel it?

LOUISA Oh yes. It is there. It is in us all. If we allow it.

Pause

RUHELA Is that all we are?
LOUISA Killers at heart?
RUHELA Is that all? *(A pause)*
LOUISA Ruhela. When you listen to the music. When you move your arms to the music. What do you feel?
RUHELA I... I...
LOUISA Is it like... flying like a bird?
RUHELA No, it's... it's... I can't put words to it.
LOUISA I'd like to know.
RUHELA *(Holds her earphones)* Well...
LOUISA Go ahead.

RUHELA puts in her earphones and turns on the CD. She stands and listens.

We hear the very end of the 'New World' Symphony. RUHELA begins to conduct. As she does so, she faces us, as if we were the orchestra.

Behind her, LOUISA picks up her suitcase. She coughs a little and pats her chest. Unseen by RUHELA she leaves slowly. The money is on the ground.

ABS and MEL enter from different directions, in jogging clothes. They meet, stop and look at each other. LOUISA turns and looks at all three.

RUHELA conducts. The Symphony ends. She bows to us. All four actors bow to us.

The End.